MELANIN IN THE WORKPLACE

By *JANAE GRIMBALL*

Copyright © 2021, Janae Grimball

Cover image: © 2021

Publisher's Note

Printed and bound in the United States of America. All rights reserved. No part of this book may be reproduced or transmitted in any form or by any means, electronic or mechanical, including photocopying, recording, or by any information storage and retrieval system except by a review who may quote brief passages in a review to be printed in a magazine, newspaper, or on the Web without permission in writing from **Janae Grimball**.

Although the author and publisher have made every effort to ensure the accuracy and completeness of information contained in this book, we assume no responsibility for errors, inaccuracies, omissions, or any inconsistency herein. Neither the publisher nor the author shall be liable for damages arising from here.

Dedications

I would like to dedicate this book to all of the people of color who came before us and paved the way so that we can be successful.

Acknowledgements

I would like to thank my husband and all of my close friends who encouraged me to write this book; you mean the world to me forever and always.

HARDWORK AND PEOPLE OF COLOR

Did you know that people of color are some of the most ambitious, hard-working, and dedicated people that exist? From the time that we are children, our families have instilled the value of hard work within us. This value signifies strength, perseverance, and resilience that we are told will help us overcome the discrimination, stereotypes, and injustice that we are born with. We are told that hard-work will break through racism, poverty, rejection and socio-economic levels.

    As people of color, we have watched our parents, grandparents, and great-grandparents exemplify this discipline through hell and high water. Going to work cleaning up after the white man, driving the white man, raising the white mans' kids, fixing the white man's possessions, and so on. Fighting through sickness, segregation, reduced wages, and lack of opportunities. All while praying that the next generation will have better chances, less adversity, and a shot at The American Dream.

    The barriers that people of color face when trying to achieve The American Dream are all different depending on their ethnicity, but these various barriers exist, nonetheless. For African Americans, the barriers began when our ancestors were stolen from their land and forced to provide free labor as slaves. For Native Americans, they began when foreigners arrived and massacred their people while stealing their land. For Latin Americans, they began when migrating to America to escape corruption but were met with ICE, detention camps, and deportation. Despite the numerous barriers, people of color work hard to overcome their circumstances in hopes of leaving a successful legacy for future generations.

Growing up as a child of color, we are often reminded of the importance of working harder than our counterparts. This is supposed to help offset the setbacks that the color of our skin has predetermined. Children of color are taught that the color of their skin may lead to discomfort, pain, injustice, and even death. This reality causes uneasiness, anxiety, and full-blown fear. Knowing that no matter how hard you work, how educated you are, or how good of a person you are, someone will define you based solely on the melanin in your skin. For many successful minorities, overcoming these barriers is what drives us to break through the circumstances and situations that life has placed upon us. But how hard does a melanated person have to work to have The American Dream? At times this can seem like an unrelenting task that will never be complete.

Hard work begins for the child of color with education. For many of us, our parents sacrificed so much and worked very hard to ensure that we have the same educational opportunities that white children have. The economic barriers that people of color face impact the quality of our education significantly. Our schools don't have the same funding which causes educational limitations. This lack of equal education led many of our parents to send us to "white" schools for better curriculums and opportunities. It is in this forum that many of us first witness white privilege and the hard work that is expected from us to just be in the same room.

  Have you ever known for certain that you studied your hardest but did not pass that test? How many times have you shown up first to practice, stayed last, and still not been chosen? A melanated person can not succeed in any capacity in America without hard work. We must work hard to stay alive, be accepted, be invited, and be understood. We must be mild-mannered, politically correct and culturally detached all before our hard work towards education and careers even begin. What does this do to our mindset towards hard-work if we are facing a mountain of barriers, to begin with?

Many people of color fall prey to society's plot to keep us marginalized. The truth is for some people of color no matter how hard they work they won't be able to overcome the generational curse of poverty, disparaging neighborhoods, and poor education. Many people of color believe the trap of The American Dream is that you will actually be successful with hard-work alone. I am here to tell you that for all of the hard-working generations that people of color have given, our success has been rationed to us like bread in a soup kitchen.

For our elders, the opportunities of today did not exist but they prepared us to be hard workers for when opportunities present themselves. However, they could not prepare us for what lies on the other end of the acceptance to that college, career, team, etc. What to expect when you have "made it". It's over right? If you are like me, you believed that once you got that degree or made it to that position you would be seen as equal, treated fairly, and accepted. No more judgment because of my skin color. No more snide comments about ignorance or laziness because I am here with you, working even harder and I have proven myself, right? People of color have achieved great feats over the decades and civil rights organizations like the NAACP and Black Lives Matter have magnified the excessive struggles we face. However, little is still done today about melanin in the workplace.

NO CULTURE ALLOWED

Many of us are familiar with the recent viral video of a young Latino high school student so proud that he is the first in his family to graduate high school that he draped the Mexican flag over his shoulder to represent his heritage. As he approached the principal to receive his high school diploma he was met with rejection due to "violating school policy". The young man was eventually given his diploma but it was a huge conversation starter about how society has ostracized people of color by using "policies" to restrict the cultural affiliation of minorities.

This type of ultimatum is not new and has been occurring as long as integration and equal rights have been implemented. The culture of a person not only includes ethnic religion and practices, but the way we dress and even communicate is as unique as our melanated skin. It tells a story of our ancestors and our current perception of the world around us. From the black womans' gold plated hoop earrings to the middle eastern womans' hijab; culture and people of color are one and the same. So why is it that society has implemented policies that negatively associate our culture with unprofessionalism?

    My first experience with this came in high school in Tallahassee, FL. I loved to write with those big puffball pens that came in different colors. While in my white teachers' class, I pulled out my pen to take notes as she had instructed. She approached me and said, "You need to get something more appropriate to write with." I was shocked but remained respectful in my reply, " This is all I have to write with, and what's wrong with this? " I said timidly. "You are distracting the class and if you do not have anything else, you need to leave my class now!" I was taken aback by her demeanor but I knew that with the sternness in her voice, she meant it. I packed my bag, left the class for the day, and never wrote with those pens ever again. Not only did I miss an important lesson in class that day, but it also taught me an even bigger lesson. If I wanted to be in her class learning like everyone else, I had to tone down the way I expressed my uniqueness. This may seem small and insignificant to some, but for people of color, we know better.

    School is the first introduction we have to the outside world. As we get older, it prepares us to enter the workforce by teaching us education, social skills, and how to follow rules. On the first day of school, we receive handbooks that tell us the school code and the rules students are expected to follow. Rules like: No sagging pants, no head coverings, no piercings, etc. seem to target cultural expressions associated with people of color. Early on we get the message that when we are in places outside of our community, we have to dress, speak, and behave the way they have instructed in order for us to be there. Once we are in the safety of our own home, we are free to express our culture. This conditioning equips us to accept what is coming once we go out into the world. How many times have you heard that long nails, certain hair colors, or hairstyles are against "policy"?

When I was twenty-four, I was given an opportunity to be a manager at a popular soup and salad restaurant. The franchise owner was a black man and I was excited about joining the team. As a black woman, we express ourselves with nails, jewelry, and most importantly our hair. At the time the artist K. Michelle was popular as well as her bright red hair color. I loved it! I had my hair colored red and got a sew-in with the matching hair color. The next day I went to work and received many compliments from customers about how great it looked. However, I noticed the white supervisors in the corner whispering to one another. I did not know why but I continued to work as usual. That weekend I was surprised when I received a call from human resources. She had a screenshot from one of the cameras in the restaurant of my hair color and informed me that I could not return to work until my hair was black. I was devastated! Not only had I spent a lot of money to get my hair done, but I also did not have money to re-do my hair so soon. What did my hair color have to do with my work ethic? What did my hair color have to do with my performance or customer service? I remember thinking about how the redhead white girl would never get this call.

 So what did I do? I borrowed money from my mom, went to the beauty supply store and bought a box of black dye, and changed my hair color. The next day when I went to work, one of the white supervisors came up to me and said, "I see you changed your hair." I held my head high and said "Oh yes! That style was old!" To keep my dignity, I pretended as if the choice was mine alone. Little did I know millions of people of color all over the United States were struggling with that same issue and they still are today. Natural hair, braids, locs, and colored hair are all synonymous with blacks and are all deemed unprofessional.

    Some people might ask, "why didn't you just quit!". One thing my mother always taught me is that if you wanna get where you want to be you have to play the game. When faced with this type of adversity, I adapted because I knew my goals were bigger than a chain soup and salad restaurant. They were just a stepping stone to the bigger picture I had envisioned for myself but the stone was still needed at the time. Like everything in my life, I looked at that experience as a lesson. From then on, for every job I made sure to take the time to familiarize myself with their policies. Why? Because you can not question what you don't know about. Had I read their policy manual, I would have known that the policy stated specifically no unnatural hair colors were allowed. Red is not an unnatural hair color so therefore they would have had to allow me to wear it or make a policy change. Always familiarize yourself with the company's handbook. This will be your Bible in a sense because it will help you dodge a lot of your white counterparts' attempts to bend rules so that you do not fit.

    Unfortunately, people of color not only have to worry about their hair when in the workplace. Our names, accents, and dress present barriers for us that we are forced to try to water down to make society feel comfortable. Have you ever had a white person mispronounce your name? Did you correct them? Our names speak to our heritage and culture and represent who our parents destined us to be, they hold power! There is nothing wrong with a polite correction when someone mispronounces it.

  One of the biggest burdens people of color face while in the workplace is in the way we speak. Cultural stereotypes have hung over us like a black cloud, even when we are educated we somehow still feel the need to erase our cultural tone in the workplace. For some of us it's to sound "professional", for others it's in an attempt to avoid the clichéd dialogue with our white counterparts. You know the random 'hola' to you when everyone else receives a hello, or the "what's up dog". Yes, the same company that said you can not wear your African head-wrap has employees who are brazen enough to appropriate your culture right in your face.

In 2019, I thought I made it to my dream job after achieving my bachelor's degree in Psychology. I was working as a forensic interviewer in a predominately white county and I had never felt more unsure of myself. Soon I found myself in a room full of district attorneys, law enforcement, and several other agencies. I was speaking on a subject, and my director, yep you guessed it a white woman, said to my co-worker "Wow, she is very well-spoken." My first thought was, "oh what a nice compliment." But after thinking about it further, I questioned - "I am very well spoken? As opposed to who or what? What did she expect me to sound like? Would she have been as surprised by this from my non-black co-worker?"

By this point, I was not only used to seeing this in my personal experiences but with other people of color that I knew in the workplace as well. I had a co-worker who was amazing at her job and was an even more wonderful person. She was a Muslim black woman. She asked me to be a reference for her with some jobs she was applying to, of course, I said "Sure, absolutely!" I remember getting a call from the human resources department at the job she really wanted. I made sure to give her rave reviews and after speaking to the woman it sounded like the job was hers. After all, she had more than the education and experience they were requiring!

 About a week later, I checked in with her to see if she had heard anything from the job. "Yeah, I did not get the position," she said barely above a whisper. "What!" I shouted in disbelief, how is that possible? I pondered this the rest of the day, how did she not get that job? She was qualified, interviewed well, and even had great reviews from her references. I started wondering if it was her hijab. And I could not help but question, would she have gotten the job if she had not been wearing it?

It's no question that Middle Eastern people of color have been stereotyped as terrorists after September 11, 2001, when the Twin Towers were attacked. I remember it vividly, although I was only in the 6th grade at the time. We had a few Muslim kids at our school, after the attack I saw white students throwing batteries at their heads in the hallway. This was while our white teachers stood by, watched, and did nothing. I could not believe the ignorance and I was even more disappointed at the teachers who seemed to get joy out of the assault, instead of protecting all students. After that day I never saw the Muslim students again at school and I have always wondered how that impacted their lives.

Have you ever had an amazing phone interview and showed up to the in-person interview and received stares or heard whispers about your Religion? Wondering to yourself if I represent my culture will they think I am a terrorist? Will they bully me? Will they understand Ramadan and its significance to my life? We all know the cliché answer that no job can "discriminate" against anyone's race, religion, or gender. But when it comes to people of color we know better. I am here to tell you that your culture belongs in the workplace! Wear your hijab, turban, native dress! Place that prayer rug in your office and use it! It is only when white people are face to face with our cultures that they can begin to understand them. That is why they work so hard to prevent culture in the workplace.

PRO.FES.SION.AL.ISM

The word *professionalism* is a word that people of color need to pick apart and digest. Who determines what is professional or not? Professionalism has been defined as "the competence or skill expected of a professional." What does this mean for people of color? And how is it that no matter what we do we end up finding ourselves with two additional letters in front of this word? (UN-PROFESSIONAL)

I am here to tell you that the foundation of the word ties back to our history and is the very reason it still never quite fits. You see, people of color were never meant to be professionals in the United States. White people never intended for us to have any competence and certainly not skills! We have all seen the Disney movie Pocahontas and how the colonizers referred to the Native Americans as savages. How many of us sang-a-long as a child "Savages, Savages, barely even human"! Of course, as children, it went right over our head that they were talking about ALL people of color native to their lands.

 Or how about the fact that still today Native Americans are held on reservations, living in poverty and often forced to choose between their heritage or becoming "Americanized". Recently, Native Americans have been making huge progress towards shedding light on the conditions and lack of resources on the reservations. We can not even begin to address the unequal rights of African Americans without starting with the historical and continuous unjust and genocide of the Native Americans! Next, all we have to do is look at how and why Africans were brought to America and we know what they intended for us. I am sorry to say it was never to be doctors, lawyers, presidents, scientists, or mathematicians. It was for free labor but I am pleased to say that people of color always rise above preconceived determinations!

    Certain careers may dictate a specific type of dress, hairstyle, and even the way we speak. If you are desiring to be an attorney, your everyday work attire may be a suit or a blazer with a conservative skirt with your hair tucked back or cleanly shaven. You may remember a commercial that came on a while back that showcased a white man dressed as a disc jockey and a black man in a suit claiming to be a tax professional. When asked who the people would trust with their money, they all said the black man who was not a tax professional but a disc jockey in real life. We all judge people by their appearances. It's a natural instinct, but for people of color, it is often that we are stereotyped as being unprofessional or less trustworthy than our counterparts. The uncomfortable truth is if you are a black attorney wearing your nicest suit to court, there are still some people who will view you as the defendant and not the litigator. Have you ever had a judge or the opposing attorney ask you "where is your lawyer"? Only to look dazed and confused when you boldly announce that you are the attorney. Have you had a customer ask to speak to a supervisor only for them to look bewildered when you boldly announce you are the supervisor? I am here to tell you that no matter what profession people of color choose, we will always be thought of by some as unprofessional or untrustworthy. So, no problem right? As long as we are always professional and don't play into our cultural stereotypes in the workplace, our counterparts will also be professional to us, right?

No, no matter how "professional" we are, we are still seen as less than by some white people people in the workplace. So what can we do? Document, document, document. My mother always told me that you can get further with a pen and paper then you can with your mouth. You see white people know that people of color are very passionate. When we believe in something or feel wronged we express it, strongly, and they love to use that to their advantage. When I was eighteen, I got a job as a cashier at the commissary (a grocery store for people in the military) in Alabama. One of my supervisors was a black woman who was always nice and professional. One day, another cashier was checking out an older white woman who was trying to pay for her groceries with a check. For some reason, the system was not taking the check so the cashier called for a supervisor to assist. The black supervisor with her same grace and poise, came over to help but the elderly white woman was irate and impatient. Suddenly, out of nowhere, the white woman yelled, "Where do they breed you niggers!"

We all froze as we watched our supervisor erupt in anger and disbelief. She began to yell and curse at the woman in disgust by her vile words. To all of us, she was justified! However, to upper management this type of response would not be tolerated, was unprofessional and no customer would be spoken to that way. She was terminated immediately and it sent shockwaves through the store. You see some white people intentionally seek to get reactions out of people of color to get us to disqualify ourselves. In the workplace, you must document every interaction that you feel to be inappropriate. Log the date and time and keep this log to establish a record.

This is especially important when your counterpart is trying to establish that you have poor work performance. Always communicate your tasks via email and limit verbal conversations because they can be altered, emails are receipts of follow-up and correspondence. I am here to tell you, never take shortcuts with white people in the workplace. Always follow all policies and procedures to a T! It seems to be okay for them to bend the rules when they please, but because of the melanin in your skin the same behavior could cost you everything you have worked for.

    We all saw the spectacle that Donald Trump carried on while in the White House pretending to be this country's leader. This powerful white man could incite violence while serving as president, meanwhile, a humble and hardworking historic Black president was harassed and publicly villainized for not producing his birth certificate to the public. If President Barack Obama and first lady Michelle Obama taught people of color anything it is the mantra, "When they go low we go high!"

It takes a lot of discipline and control of your emotions to not respond to that rude comment, unfair treatment, and micro-management. Work on this now, because when it happens you want to be prepared. Keep in mind your goals, what do you want to achieve? Is this job a stepping stone to your bigger picture? Is this the career you always dreamed of? If so, do not let anyone deter you from what you believe in and work hard for! I am here to tell you that there will be days that you may think about quitting, you may even break down and feel drained. Being around white people in the workplace can be exhausting and they will never understand how their privilege and ignorance of other cultures make people of color feel. I realized the more time I spent with them in the workplace, the more I became aware that some of them do not even know when they are doing it. I am here to tell you that you will have to allow some things to roll off of your back just to function peacefully in the workplace. But never compromise your integrity, beliefs, or character!

CODE-SWITCHING

Our culture is ingrained to the core of who we are and every time we walk through our employer's doors, it can feel like we are forced to put our true identity on pause until it's time to clock out. Our language and how we communicate with each other is very different from how we communicate with people outside of our culture. Code-switching is when people of color switch the way they speak, act, and interact with colleagues within the companies they work for. This is something we naturally adjust to in order to function successfully in the work environment, a survival tactic so to speak. For many of us we do it so often it almost seems subconscious.

How many times has a white co-worker greeted you and you responded with "Hello, how are you doing today!" In a tone that is not quite you? Now, how many times has a co-worker from the same ethnicity greeted you and you responded with " Hey girl!" or "What's up" in your authentic voice. I'm here to tell you that our ability to dialogue comfortably in the workplace can be very limited. From the way we pronounce our words to the tone of voice we use in the workplace, we are often being judged by our counterparts. To be an educated person of color seems to come with the requirement that we must showcase our education in the workplace to show that we are not ignorant or less than. Speaking "proper" English is one way to let our counterparts know we are educated, but code-switching allows us to blend who we are with who we are pressured to be in the workplace.

    In 2018, I worked in a domestic violence shelter and the majority of my co-workers were African Americans like myself. However, we had one white co-worker who did not seem to have a lot of interaction with people of color. One day we were in the office talking and laughing with one another when she came running into the office with this look of panic and concern on her face. "Is everything alright?!" She asked, looking worried. We all looked at one another with confusion and replied "Nothing's wrong, we are just talking." She sighed with relief and said, "Oh, I heard loud shouting and I thought someone was arguing!" We all rolled our eyes and continued to talk amongst ourselves. The fact that the sound of Black women talking and laughing together sounded fearful to her was crazy to me and I have never understood it. I honestly had to chuckle to myself as I thought about the movie Bad Boys with Martin Lawerence and Will Smith. In the scene where they go to the white suspect's house, Martin tells Will, "You can't talk with all that bass in your voice, that scares white people, you have to sound like them" as he proceeds to announce himself in a white country accent.

    Code-switching is very familiar to us blacks and it is something most people of color engage in in the workplace. A recent poll I conducted determined that Asian Americans and Latin Americans also felt the need to code-switch in the workplace. Why, though? It is because code-switching makes us feel safe and inconspicuous when we are in spaces where we are the minority. I would tell myself my melanin stands out enough that I don't need my accent or loud passionate voice to make them reconsider my presence. Growing up my mother often used what we would jokingly call her "white people voice" while at work and handling business. Her tone of voice would get higher and bigger words were used for simple statements. I learned from observing her that when speaking with white people my natural voice may not be accepted and that I may appear more relatable to them if I changed it. As I made my way through college and into the workforce I realized that not all people of color used a "white people voice". I observed the looks, eye rolls, and frowns that were given to them by white people when speaking in their natural tone. It was as if they were confirming the stereotypes and justifying them.

During my time as a forensic interviewer, I worked with many multidisciplinary partners in a rural county. The director of the Division of Family and Children Services was an African American woman who left no question about who she was. From her rolling neck to speaking with her hands she was authentically herself in every way. I sort of admired her while being afraid for her at the same time. One day during a multidisciplinary meeting she was speaking very passionately about an injustice that was being done by law enforcement to a child. She was not shy or apprehensive about letting them know exactly how she felt! During the meeting, she had to step out to take a phone call and the room that was filled with white people people couldn't wait to start talking. "She's so aggressive!" "I do not like the way she intimidates others when speaking!" I sat there puzzled, I was proud of her for standing up and speaking the truth because she was right in everything she said! And quite frankly their asses needed to be called out. But at the same time what I saw as passion our cohorts saw as aggression and intimidation. When we returned to our office, my director wanted to continue the conversation. "I am going to report her to the head of DFCS, and try to get her removed from her duties!" I sat there in silence and thought to myself, this is why I will never let them see the "REAL" me. Why is it that every other culture has to understand them, but no significant attempts are made to understand other cultures? I guess that's because most rules in society are dictated by the experiences of white people.

Code-switching is a survival technique, a tool that minorities use to fit into social and professional situations. Many people of color code switch to avoid the very stereotypes that were placed on that DFCS director. Like speaking softly to avoid being labeled loud or argumentative. Although code-switching helps us fit into a space that was not designed for us it has many drawbacks. Have you ever felt tired of pretending to speak or behave differently than you do in private? I have, and to be honest, I have been code-switching so long that it has become a part of me. One minute I am using my natural voice tone and the next I am speaking like a high society southern belle. Hell, I even do it when I am around other people of color in the workplace with whom I am not familiar. Deep down I tell myself, "I am not sure of their title or position, so I am going to present myself this way until I am positive they can be trusted with my true self." Another downside to code-switching is that even when you find those co-workers with whom you can be your authentic self with you still have to monitor your interactions with them in the workplace so that you don't tip off your outside coworkers.

 Most white people do not know we code switch and of course have never had to do it themselves because all forums cater to them. One of my favorite shows, Insecure, follows a young woman named Issa and her friends who are trying to make it in Los Angeles. Issa's best friend, Molly, is an attorney working at a law firm. In one episode, it follows how a black intern comes into the law firm being her authentic self to all the other staff. Molly tries to pull her to the side to give her a heads up about toning it down a little while in mixed company. The girl becomes offended by Molly's audacity and tells her that has gotten this far in life without changing who she is. And what happens next? You guessed it, the girl was "let go" by the partners while Molly looked on in pity, we never see the intern on the show again.

You see, while it is great to have other staff to relate to in the workplace, you have to make sure that you do not become too relaxed. As soon as they observe a groupthink mentality they will disband it or worse remove you altogether. Code-switching is about balance, knowing when to let that guard down and when to leave it up. When researching the topic I ran across an article covering code-switching and why people of color use it. There was a list and it included, "to exclude others". I could not believe my eyes, I assumed whoever wrote this article is not a person of color as they obviously had no idea what they were talking about! We do not code-switch to exclude others! If anything, if they weren't so hell-bent on making every other culture assimilate to them, they would have their own culture that was unique to them. Why are two employees speaking in their native language to one another viewed as excluding others in the workplace?

People of color have our own unique speech, dialect, interpretations, and swag. It took me 31 years to finally realize that my voice tone, passionate expression, and natural way of being did not make me less than my counterparts. This melanin is a total package deal and any company that wants me gets all my flavor and my fabulous culture. I had to look at myself in the mirror and say "Yes! I am a black woman, I am of African descent, and all my nuances paint a vivid picture of that." I urge all my people of color to find that mirror and do the same. From my Latino people to my Middle Eastern people. Our Melanin is a package deal, to be handled with care and treated with the utmost respect.

CRABS IN A BARREL

With all the talk about code-switching in the workplace, I feel it is just as important to discuss the dangers that can occur amongst our own people of color in the workplace. We have all heard the term crabs in a barrel. The expression is used to depict impoverished people who pull down one of their own when they begin to thrive and overcome the same barriers holding the others down. Like crabs, they are willing to pull one of their own down so that they all can remain down together. They would rather everyone suffer than have one of their own escape.

For many of us, this is all too familiar, from the long-time "friends" who try to convince you to go back to your old ways; to the supervisor who is threatened by your potential. People of color not only face challenges in the workplace with their white adversaries, sometimes it is our own people that make the dream of having more seem unattainable. One thing I have always made sure to remember is to never assume anything of someone just because their skin tone matches mine.

    In 2017, I was a college student with my sights set on entering the world of crisis intervention. That year my boyfriend and I went to a reputable tax agency to file our taxes and was immediately greeted by a middle-aged black woman. "Hey! What's up with yall? Yall tryna file some taxes today?" At first, I was taken aback by how unprofessional she was but shrugged it off. "Yes, we have an appointment today," I said quickly. "Well look, I got the hook up on some kids if y'all need some to claim on yall taxes!" She said loudly. "Naw we good," I replied with an attitude. I was mad at the fact that she just assumed that we were into breaking the law. What made her think she could walk up to complete strangers, while she is at work and offer something so illegal? It seemed to me that if I was into that kind of thing I would want to be more discreet about it. The fact is you never know what someone's intentions are until you get to know them. This fact is never more true than in the workplace.

When coming into an organization, observing the people and how they act is your best move. This will help you determine how you too should maneuver within that environment. When I became a forensic interviewer in an organization dominated by white people, I was happy to see that one of the supervisors was another black woman. Since there were not many of us I expected her to welcome me with open arms and give me the lay of the land but she didn't. She was cold and rude, at that. She was quick to point out my mistakes while also informing the white supervisors of every little thing. Immersed in her established relationships with our counterparts, I was confused and disgusted. How could a Sistah not acknowledge another knowing that we are far and few between in this line of work? As it turns out it is not all that uncommon, be aware that with these crabs you will have to watch your step. I realized that she was intimidated by my potential and afraid that she may be replaced as the "token black girl". I always remained professional and would not dare code switch with her. As far as I was concerned she was worse than the system that our people spent their lives fighting against. Not because I expected special treatment and not because she did her job, or adhered to the rules but because she contributed to the systematic division of our people that was put in place to keep us oppressed. I am here to tell you that some people of color think that there are a limited amount of opportunities for us.

That once they have obtained a spot no other person of color can have one unless they are removed. They become territorial over their roles and positions as if it defines them. It doesn't! We are meant to help one another succeed and get ahead. Success does not belong to one group of people and most certainly does not belong to one individual. There is enough room for everyone to be successful, for everyone to eat. The sooner that people of color learn to live by this principle the sooner we can work together to tear down the barriers that have been built against us. Has another person of color ever made you feel less than or inadequate? How many times has another person of color who you looked to for guidance or mentoring disappointed you by placing their fears and negativity onto you?

    In 2015, I started a nonprofit for women to help them receive services. I was enrolled in school and my teacher at the time referred me to his sister who ran a business helping people get their 501c3 for a fee. I waited until tax time and used my refund to invest in a business for myself. While going through the process, I learned a lot and found many resources beneficial to someone looking to open a non-profit. I was looking for service providers to provide daycare to the women in my program when a woman of color direct messaged me.

"Good afternoon ma'am, I know you are looking for employees but I am interested in starting my own company and was hoping you could point me in the right direction of getting a grant?" I read her words and could feel her anxiety through the screen. Why was she so apprehensive to ask me about what services I used? Didn't she know that our businesses could both thrive and be successful? I immediately responded to her with every resource and contact I had made from the time

I started my business. Why wouldn't I? What would I gain by hindering this woman's process? I am here to tell you that if you know something that can help another person of color, share it with them! Forget all this talk about "I worked hard so should the next person!" You see one thing about white people is they love to help one another achieve greatness. A friend of a friend or a long distant cousin, it doesn't matter, a hand-up is never far away.

We as people of color have to realize that the only way for all of the crabs to get out of the barrel is if they help each other up. The entire barrel could be free if they saw past their fear of someone else obtaining what they can't. I hope that that woman's business thrived and that she paid it forward to another person of color in need. I bet that supervisor will never know how she could have positively impacted my experience at the job if she had just extended an invitation to lunch or helped me navigate the work culture. The mindset should always be that the success of one of my people is a success for me and my success means the success of another person of color.

MONEY TALKS

One of the most important decisions as a person of color in the workplace is money! For generations, our people have worked harder and longer for much less pay. We have taken jobs that were considered demeaning or less than and were still not able to fully provide for our families. While employment opportunities have seemingly opened up to all people of color, one thing that remains unchanged is the pay deficit that we receive compared to our counterparts.

Recently, the great Viola Davis spoke out about the significant pay difference that actors/actresses of color receive compared to white ones. In a 2018 interview, Davis said "I got the Oscar, I got the Emmy, I got the two Tony's, I've done Broadway, I've done off-Broadway, I've done TV, I've done films, I've done all of it. I have a career that's probably comparable to Meryl Streep, Julianne Moore, and Sigourney Weaver. They came out of Yale, they came out of Julliard, they came out of NYU. They had the same path as me, and yet I am nowhere near them, not as far as money, not as far as job opportunities, nowhere close to it."

    This powerful statement from one of the most successful women of color is gut-wrenching. That during this day and time she faces the same challenges that the beautiful Dorothy Dandridge did over fifty years ago! One thing for sure, two things for certain, people of color across all fields of employment encounter this injustice in the workplace. It is essential that when going into the workforce, people of color negotiate the pay scale for the position they are going into.

    I wonder if Viola Davis has ever asked for the same salary as Meryl Streep? Do you think she would have gotten the role? The fact is you do not know what will be given to you if you do not ask. Questions like, "What does an 'entry-level' salary look like? How often are raises and promotions given?" These are all important questions for any employee but especially people of color.Doing research on sites such as Indeed Salaries or Glassdoor can not only tell you what companies have paid entry level employees before, but you can also view reviews from previous employees about the work culture and position. Like most of us, many times I would be so eager to get the job that I did not ask the money questions. Believe me when I tell you this is a big mistake! Have you ever had a conversation with a white co-worker and found out that they are making more than you in the same position? Or accidentally stumbled upon this information?

When it comes to people of color, knowing our worth is much more than a hashtag. One major factor that people of color have to consider is their ethnicity and how it can benefit them in the workforce. Many employers want to appeal to their clientele and clients from different places all over the world just like us. They often ask you if you speak another language besides English because they want to use that to benefit their company. Have you ever been at work and a co-worker asks you to help a Spanish-speaking customer? Now of course you do not mind helping out here and there but at the end of the day are you getting paid to be a translator? Do you even feel comfortable interpreting for someone else you do not know? White people tend to group all ethnicities together and do not differentiate between ethnicities like Puerto Rican and Brazilian or African and Jamaican. However, we know the differences are huge! Starting with the fact that one culture speaks Spanish and the other speaks Portuguese.

I have witnessed Latino co-workers being asked to translate for clients and being pulled away from their assigned duties to take on additional tasks just because of their ethnicity. I am here to tell you that if you want to use your native language in the workplace make sure you are being compensated! Did you know the average pay for translators in the United States is $46,023 according to 2021 Indeed salaries? Now add up all the times you have "pitched in" to help out your co-workers with translating. Were you compensated accordingly? Probably not, it is important to discuss this with your employer if you choose to incorporate it into your job description and duties. Many employers try to cut costs by not hiring translators and hiring people of color to do all their translating. In your interview let them know that you have a native language and ask them if they intend on needing you to translate. If so, make sure to inform them of your desired salary including the service of translation. If you choose not to integrate your native language in the workplace, make sure to disclose this as well. Some people will see the culture in your name and assume you have a native language that you are fluent in and assume that you are willing to use it. There is nothing wrong with letting them know that you do not wish to integrate your native language in the workplace.

Once you have considered your ethnicity, the next thing to consider is their work environment. As people of color, we have to do our due diligence to make sure we are entering places that will not be detrimental to our mental health. Ask those hard questions in your interview. Questions like, "is there a high level of diversity within your agency? How often does your corporation complete cultural competency training?" These are the questions that will help you to gauge the company's awareness and inclusiveness.

    I am here to tell you that money will allow you to accept the job but it will not keep you there if you are in a toxic work environment! For the first time in history, the world watched as Olympic gold medalist Simone Biles and professional tennis player Naomi Osaka backed out of their commitments to take care of their mental health. As people of color, we have been conditioned to believe that our mental health does not matter, please believe me when I assure you it does. I learned the hard way that as a Black woman in a majority white woman field, I had no idea that when I accepted the position that I was going to be entering a world of highly educated women who were severely unaware of cultural competency. Being immersed in an environment full of people who could not relate to me impacted my mental health and my self-esteem.

Money cannot help you assimilate to unhealthy environments! If an employer informs you that they do not mandate cultural competency training for their staff, RUN, and do not look back! They are telling you everything you need to know in that one sentence. Once you have determined the best you can that you would like to move forward, do not settle for less! It is often difficult to jump to your desired salary once hired depending on the company's raise procedures. As people of color, we must be confident in marketing ourselves and our desired price point. Our worth is as priceless as the blood our ancestors shed. As a wise woman once said, "Know your worth and then add tax." And that is how you make your money talk!

THE SELLOUT

We all know that one person who "got ahead" in life and started to act "funny" with their own people. All of a sudden they no longer can be bothered to come around the old neighborhood or give to those around them who are less fortunate. As people of color, we are always reminded to stay true to ourselves no matter how high we climb on the ladder. But for many of us, it is a constant struggle and we hold on to the past so tightly that our growth is stunted. Why is it that people of color are expected to become successful yet not desire nice things? To work hard and give handouts to others? To code switch yet remain ourselves?

Let's be honest, it can feel like yet another burden that you inherited through your skin. As a Black woman, I remember always being aware of this looming title that hung over my head like a dark cloud. My father was an Army Sergeant and my mother, a go-getter who was determined to make it out of a small town. I was born in Germany and received dual citizenship. We never lived in my parents home town of Bradenton, Florida but I will always remember when we visited being picked on by my cousins, "Why you tryna talk white!" To me, I was talking like myself but at this young age, I realized that people of color are held to a different standard even by their own kind.

  Jokes are one thing, but the first time I ever truly felt like a sellout was in 2019 while I was working as a forensic interviewer. One of my frequent law enforcement officers came in for me to conduct an interview on a child on his caseload. Only this time, he had another officer with him who he informed was temporarily in his department observing. As always, I was kind and courteous and offered the gentleman some water and snacks. He accepted and I had no problem bringing it to him while making small talk. It was right after Thanksgiving and to make small talk I asked him about his holiday. "Oh, I went up to Kentucky to visit my family and we ate good!" He said casually. "That's good! Did you watch the football game?" I asked, jovially. "Oh No! I am not the television watching type, I like to hunt." I nodded while smiling and then left the room to begin my interview. Once we finished, my frequent attending officer told his guest that he could head out and that all he had left to do was gather paperwork. We shook hands and I showed him out, "It was nice meeting you, I hope to see you soon!" I said eagerly. Once he left, my frequent officer began to talk about how disappointed he was that the kid didn't say much. "Yea, I hate when that happens, especially when you're training a new guy," I said. The look on his face when I said that was one of surprise and shock, "He is not in training!" He said loudly, "Don't you know who that is? He was transferred to our department while he is under investigation with internal affairs! He killed a guy while on duty and is supposed to be on leave with pay! Don't you watch the news?!" My mouth was on the floor, for one, no I do not watch the news, and two why was he working in the first place! I quickly gathered his paperwork and got him out the door while trying to remove the shocked look from my face.

  Before they could barely reach the steps out of the building I pulled out my phone and Googled the incident. Sure enough there it was! Officer shoots and kills a black homeless man. I hesitated to hit play on the news clip video but couldn't stop myself. And there, on video was the footage of a black man in his car while police surrounded him in their vehicles.

The officer yells "get out of the car!" and at the same time, as he is speaking, he is pulling the trigger shooting through his own windshield and into the windshield of the black man hitting him directly in the eye. The same guy that I had just shaken hands with, got a drink of water for and had a friendly conversation with, was responsible for killing one of my people! I never felt so disgusted in my life! "Am I a sellout?!" I kept saying to myself over and over. I went home and crawled up into a ball on the floor sobbing uncontrollably. For the first time, I felt like the work I was doing was against my culture, against my people.

    Unfortunately for me that feeling only got worse as 2020 came along and more murders of black people sparked protests all over the state of Georgia. As a forensic interviewer, it was my job to work with law enforcement and the district attorney's office. However, as a woman of color, I felt so disgusted to have to laugh and joke and pretend to be okay with the police when I wasn't! I kept telling myself I won't talk politics at work or engage in any conversations about what is happening in the outside world. But the boldest ones would come right in my office and start complaining about the protests! "I am so sick of these people protesting, I have to work double hours because of it!" They would say to me. I could not believe they even had the nerve to complain to me about it! Did they think I was on their side? It bothered me a lot. Mostly because I could not speak out about how I felt about the murders of my people. HR never sent out an email to check in on their staff of color or to say we stand with people of color!

    I am here to tell you the workplace is one of the worst places to have to go to when your people are being crucified weekly. How are we supposed to act? What can you say when agitators confront you? Are you a sellout for not cursing them out? Like most people of color in the workplace, these same questions ran through my mind. The answer soon after became very clear to me with another question. Why am I here? I asked myself, what is my purpose behind being at this job and where did it fit in my plan to achieve my goals? You see, asking yourself why will always help you to find your foundation. I knew that I needed to be quiet, stay firm, and be patient until I could transition. Don't get me wrong, I wanted to speak up but I knew I was not emotionally capable of doing so in a work-appropriate manner. I had other co-workers of color who were able to dialogue with law enforcement and articulate themselves appropriately. But I was not in that space at that time.

You see, the term sellout is defined as "A person who betrays something to which he or she is said to owe allegiance." People of color in the workplace must understand what I had to learn. You are not a sell-out because you worked hard, because you moved out of the old neighborhood, because you outgrew those stagnant friends, or because you remained quiet for a time being. You are not a sell-out because you did your job or told your twice removed uncle no this time when he asked to borrow fifty bucks. As long as you know your why and your integrity is intact, I give you permission to release the dark cloud of fear that is attached to the word sellout. Something our melanin can not dictate for us are the choices we make. We as individuals have power over that. And in life as well as business the choices we make today determine our future tomorrow!

THE COLOR OF INSECURITY

As people of color, we have endured an unhealthy daily dose of hate, rejection, persecution, and ridicule. All of our lives we have been forced to see our people enslaved, imprisoned, massacred, and impoverished. After being told you are not good enough for so long anyone will start to believe it. I am here to tell you that the color of insecurity is black and brown. All those insecurities that have been poured into us seep into our melanated skin like the toxin it is and does what toxins do, destroy. No matter how long ago our oppression was, we are never too far removed from the internal damage caused. The fears of our parents and grandparents are now the insecurities we have within us today. Growing up, I always had this fear of white people especially when I was the only person of color in the room. To be honest I don't know where this fear stemmed from. I've had it for as long as I could remember.

    When I was eleven, I had a white friend that lived in my neighborhood. We played together often and even spent the night at each other's houses. One day her father asked me if I wanted to attend the youth group retreat with their church. I had been to the Sunday service before and knew that there was a black boy who also attended the church so I said yes. When we got to the retreat, imagine my surprise when he was nowhere to be found. An intense panic came over me. I tried to ignore it but then my friend began to act differently around the other white kids. I felt so inferior and inadequate next to all of them. I broke down crying and told her father I wanted to go home because I was afraid. He seemed surprised and ran off to speak with the other adults. After that, everyone at the retreat was super nice to me, too nice. You can tell that word had gotten around to be extra sweet to the negro girl because she is afraid. From then on, I made sure to limit my presence in places where I would be outnumbered as the only minority.

Whenever I walked into a place where I am outnumbered, my anxiety would immediately kick in and the insecurities start. I would tell myself "I don't belong here and I don't fit in." At times I would even tell myself, "They don't really like you, they are pretending." Now ask yourself, do you have any insecurities that arise when you are the minority in a space? If so, it is important to address them so that you can go into any place or situation with your head held high. I learned the hard way by not addressing my insecurity when it first began.

When I started my job as a forensic interviewer, all of those insecurities manifested themselves into anxiety and discomfort. I had so many insecurities from how I dressed, how I wore my hair, all the way to how well I did my job. It was clear that my insecurities were revealing themselves one by one. And whatever wasn't in my head the toxic work environment added to. It wasn't until I began telling myself that I am good enough, I deserve to be here, and that they are not better than me that I began to release some of my insecurities.

  You see, we as people of color have to give ourselves permission to be accepted. So what if your natural hair is big and kinky, so what if your accent is heavy, so what if your cultural dress is different from everyone else? We do not have to make ourselves smaller to fit into their world. Many of us have insecurities about different things for different reasons. A very good friend of mine shared with me that when she finished college and entered the workplace her biggest insecurity was her hair.

Now you would never guess this if you saw her because her hair is literally the most beautiful mix of texture, size, and curls. But for her, she thought it was not appropriate. She only felt comfortable when it was pulled back in a bun or a low ponytail so that she looked more professional. It was not until a new black supervisor was hired who arrived with a long beautiful natural blowout, looking more professional than our other coworkers, that she saw a representation of herself. She was able to express to her supervisor how she always had an insecurity about her hair and the supervisor taught her something that she will always carry with her. She told her that our natural hair is as beautiful as their natural hair and that she should be proud of it! Representation matters! We need to see versions of ourselves in all shapes, sizes, styles, and careers. You never know how you overcoming your insecurities can inspire the next person to overcome theirs.

Let's be honest, some of our insecurities come from toxic environments and upbringings that have contributed to us not feeling enough. People who are raised by love are healthier overall than those who are raised in survival mode. Past traumas and toxic attachment styles have to be addressed because if they don't you will carry that bias into your career. The things we tell ourselves will manifest themselves into reality. Toxic work environments do exist. From the job that only has people of color working in the back or night shift, to that supervisor who always makes snide comments about your work, to the coworker who just has to inform everyone that you are five minutes late. A toxic work environment will all but ensure that your underlying insecurities, as well as new ones, will come out. Have you ever left work feeling emotionally exhausted or borderline depressed? Was it the job itself or the people you were working with? I realized that I was in a toxic work environment when my insecurities began to grow. I couldn't be two minutes late for our morning meeting without being talked about. I could not voice my concerns without being judged. I could not be myself without worrying that my statements were being taken the wrong way.

    It got to the point where I was eating lunch in my car or my office alone. Sure, I had some insecurities that I bought along with me, but I had never been insecure about who I am as a person! It had gotten so bad that I was going into the restroom turning on the faucet and crying my eyes out. Work felt like a high school popularity contest rather than a professional setting. I needed that reassurance from my peers to let me know that I was valued and appreciated. Having a therapist will help you navigate the challenges of worklife and entrepreneurship. It will also help you to have positive mental health, heal from generational curses, and trauma. I am here to tell you that if your job does not reassure you or make you feel comfortable honey you are going to have to do it yourself! Going to counseling regularly is an outlet to use to build your self-esteem and reduce your insecurities. They do not get to disrupt our emotional stability or add to our insecurities. As people of color, we deserve healthy environments, regular self-care, and healthy self esteems!

PLAYING THE GAME

With all the talk about the barriers people of color face in the workplace I felt it is important to discuss how we overcome them. You see, when you are interacting with coworkers you must "play the game." This helped me to thrive in my career as I learned how to adapt to any and every situation I was faced with. The toxic work environment from the last chapter taught me so much about fitting into spaces that were not designed for me. Whether you are running your own business or working for someone else, adaptation and flexibility are essential to a successful career.

I credit my understanding of that to my first supervisor at my first job in my field. Never underestimate the importance of a great mentor, they truly help you to grow and develop. Once I became a forensic interviewer and realized I was in a field with limited diversity, I knew I had to sit back and observe. Observe how they treated each other as well as themselves. It wasn't long until I realized that everyone was on edge, afraid to be talked about by another, and overly judgemental. I knew I had to be careful of how I carried myself, as well as how I interacted with them. Imagine my surprise to see these "well-to-do" white women cursing in professional settings and making inappropriate jokes internally as well as externally. I remember I called my mom my first week and told her all about it. She said, "Don't you do that, it's okay when they do it but if you lose their respect, your outcome won't be the same as theirs." That really made me think, how would I be perceived if I walked into the room cursing about clients and community partners? I always spoke intelligently and with a calm tone when around them. I never gossiped or indulged in vulgar casual conversation. You see, when we are in spaces that were not designed for us, in order to stay there, we must follow all the rules, make very few mistakes, and be better than everyone else. Back in the day, our elders would say keep your head down, shut up, and do your job. I always did my job with the utmost integrity, never taking shortcuts or violating policy. I made sure during my training period that I purchased a big notepad so that as I was being given instructions I could write them down so I didn't have to go back and ask the same question again.

    One of the biggest assets of playing the game is documentation. One day I was sitting in my office when an email came through from my supervisor asking me to upload my documents into the database. Red flag! My first thought was, why is she sending me an email for something that could have been a quick statement to my face? Then it hit me, she wanted to have proof that it was not complete, and if left that way she could have proof that she requested it. I quickly emailed her back, "Hi, thank you for following-up with me about those documents. They are currently in the process of being uploaded and should show in about five minutes on your end! Please feel free to reach out to me if you have any additional questions/concerns." You see, in the workplace, an email is so much more than just an email. As my mentor supervisor taught me, anything written down is a big deal as it is final and can't be redacted. If someone says you said something, that could easily be up for debate but if they have your words in writing that is what we call receipts! When faced with issues and unfair treatment, documenting the date and time along with details of the incident is the best way to handle issues that may need to go to human resources. I learned this from my encounter with a self-proclaimed redneck cop who I had to work with.

Every morning when I got to work I would lotion my hands with my scented lotion as a way to prepare myself for my day. It was never a problem, until one day while my supervisor was present she said: "Can you go wash your hands, that smell is giving me a headache and I get migraines." I was taken aback that she had the nerve to say that but nonetheless I responded with "It's no problem I can actually just leave the room because I won't be conducting the interview for you today." Now you would think that would have been good enough but no she said "No, I do not want you to leave the room I want you to go wash your hands and come back!" The look of shock on my face was far from subtle as I realized my supervisor was just staring at me. I swallowed my anger and said "Sure, no problem!" It took everything in me not to go off and say how I really felt because, to be honest, this lady chain-smoked cigarettes, and every time she came into my office the smell would be horrible. However, I had enough professionalism to not say anything and simply spray my office with an air freshener when she left. I took that moment for what it was and that is a test to see if I would come out of my character. I'm here to tell you that there is nothing our counterparts love to do more than to see what you're made of. If you're going to break down, get mad, or get loud. Will you forget where you are and lose control? Nope! Not me, I knew that I could not let this woman break me. Believe me y'all she tried from her snarky comments about my work performance to walking into my office saying "Whew honey what are you going to do with that hair of yours!" That's right, this woman came for my locs! I quickly asked "Excuse me, what did you just say?" with enough bass in my voice for her to know I wanted her to repeat it so I could immediately file a complaint with her Sergeant. She knew how to play the game though, she didn't repeat it.

  Knowing when to speak and when not to speak was my biggest lesson in playing the game. Some meetings require your observation more than anything while others are the platform for you to vocalize your knowledge. I always read the room and watched my supervisor's cues before interjecting into the conversation. Another lesson I learned from my previous mistakes. When I was working as a case manager in a domestic violence shelter, a resident was being asked to leave due to breaking the shelter rules. As her case manager, my presence was requested by my supervisor. After she was told she was being asked to leave immediately, I felt that the conversation was a bit harsh and I wanted to let her know I would still help her. "Yes, but do not worry I will still help you to find housing just give me a call!" I said eagerly. All the staff in the room got very quiet. Imagine my surprise when my supervisor called me into her office to reprimand me for speaking out of turn and promising shelter resources to a non-resident. Sometimes you will make mistakes, and maybe even get into trouble but you have to take those lessons and learn from them!

  Have you ever been reprimanded by your supervisor but felt that you were right? I have, but accepting critiques with a positive attitude will be your best friend, it's also a part of playing the game. One of my favorite quotes says "If you cannot control your emotions, you cannot control your money" by Warren Buffett. I am here to tell you that if people of color don't play the game we don't get the money. We don't get to speak disrespectfully to others, have a poor performance, or have bad customer service and keep our jobs.

Your relationship with your supervisor will be a significant factor in your success or failure. Have you had a supervisor that you loved and got along with? Now how much did you enjoy your job? Have you had a supervisor who you did not care for? Now how much did you enjoy your job? Bad leadership is always the foundation to a bad work environment and at times your success in your career seems tethered to them. Cultivate that relationship as much as you can professionally. At the end of the day, we are all humans, and as people of color, we can always make ourselves more relatable to the opposite race by using conversation starters about family, love, and food. This is a language that everyone speaks! If it can't be done, just know that now you know how to play the game and keep your head up and use it as a stepping stone to your next level!

ENTREPRENEUR-NOTS

For many people of color, entrepreneurship is the best way to obtain the goals and success they desire. That regular nine to five doesn't cut it nor does it allow for the creativity that we need to feel fulfilled and inspired. To run your business successfully is one of the most difficult objectives anyone can aspire to take on especially for people of color. But when done correctly we have seen there are no limits or ceilings on success. Just take a look at people like Daymond John, Sofia Vergara, Henry Red Cloud, and Jason Njoku.

These days anyone can hop online and start a business with social media sites like Instagram and TikTok spearheading the marketing front. With success a few clicks away, who needs a degree to be successful? You see, our white counterparts have been taught business savvy since they were children by their bank owner father or CEO grandfather. They have been shown, up close and personal, how businesses run, how to build the infrastructure, and most importantly how to obtain capital to get and keep it running. That is if the business hasn't been handed down to them altogether. Don't get me wrong, there is nothing wrong with educating your children about business. However, for people of color, we rarely have access to such premium information. Our parents and grandparents taught us how to survive to ensure our safety with little time left for sales and stocks!

    In 2015, I decided to start a non-profit to serve women in need of services. My organization was called Independence Outreach for Women Inc. I just knew I was gonna change lives while becoming very successful. The next Susan G. Coleman I told myself. I got my 501c3 and hit the ground running and I'm sad to say I didn't get very far. I did not know anything about running a non-profit. I did not know you need capital to operate and then grants to keep your organization going. You see, you can know how to produce the product you are selling but that is only a small part in comparison to being a business owner as a whole.

Many people think being an entrepreneur is an easy way out. Unaware that the hours are longer and go far beyond a typical 8 hour business day. I was working full-time when I started my organization and quickly realized that it would require more than nights and weekends to get things off of the ground. I also realized that the people I thought would help me were not as committed as I was and I was going to need to learn on my own. I have to admit, I was not only unprepared for the demands of being an entrepreneur but I was also un-knowledgeable about how to run a business. A recent article study by the Network Journal found that although thousands of minority entrepreneurs launch businesses every year, over 20 percent fail within the first year. And only 50 percent make it to the 5 year mark. Have you ever shopped black-owned to help give back to the black community but your item was poorly provided, overpriced, and worst of all poor customer service was received? If only that small business owner had taken a business administration class to help them learn about overhead, product production, customer service, and accounting. No, you don't always need those things to start your business or to have sales. You need them for longevity and to keep those customers coming back to your business.

  Maybe that's why African American entrepreneur mogul, Daymond John, teaches business classes for up-and-coming entrepreneurs. Like anything in life, if you want to be the best at it you have to practice, study, and learn the ins and outs. Successful entrepreneurs do not just lean on their own understanding, they tap into the resources around them to gain the knowledge they need to be successful. Attending workshops and seminars is a great way to gain additional business savvy and invest back into yourself. Successful entrepreneurs do not refuse an opportunity to learn and grow, and successful entrepreneurs most definitely do not become combative when constructively critiqued. If you have a bad experience with a customer, it is your responsibility to be professional. There is nothing more distasteful than a business owner speaking negatively about their own customers. I'm here to tell you that people of color must know the entrepreneur-nots so that they can get one step closer to building generational wealth!

A 2018 Bloomberg article, covered a study conducted in New Orleans that explored the difficulties that people of color face as entrepreneurs seeking lines of credit compared to white entrepreneurs. In the study, A black business owner with a business credit score of 720 went to three different banks to retrieve a business loan and was denied by all three banks. The white business owner also went to obtain a business loan but had a much lower business credit score. He did not have to go to three banks, as he walked out of the first bank with a million-dollar line of credit for his business! I want you to read that again. I wonder if that black businessman was ever able to get the capital raised or if that ended his dream of entrepreneurship? I am here to tell you that if your skin is any shade other than white, in America obtaining a loan from the bank to start your business may seem more than impossible. What I didn't know was that the majority of minority business owners start their businesses with money they have saved or from their support system. You might be saying "But what if all the people I know have the crab in the barrel mentality?" Well, then it is time for you to network, network, network!

Networking is the entrepreneur of color's best friend. Networking opportunities like attending pop-up-shops, conferences, and social media groups provide a wealth of information for entrepreneurs to have access to resources they normally would not. Jay-Z once said, "You should have at least one millionaire in your contacts." It may take some time but you will be surprised how people you meet along the way support you more than those you have known your whole life. I did not learn what I needed to know about entrepreneurship until I decided to dissolve my non-profit. I never count it as a loss but as a valuable lesson that I will keep with me.

Yes, being an entrepreneur is hard and as a person of color, you can expect it to be even harder. Yes, running a business is stressful and difficult and as a person of color, you can expect it to be even more challenging. Like I mentioned before, our melanin has predetermined a lot of things for us but as long as we invest, first in ourselves, then in our products, the rest is sure to come.

Melanin How To's

Melanin in the workplace indicates our culture, way of being, and pride that we bring effortlessly to any environment we enter. The history our melanin has is what makes us who we are and we should be proud to embrace that. Navigating working in America as a person of color can be difficult, and full of highs and lows. Although we may not all have the same experiences, it is my hope that you can be aware of what others like you have gone through and grow from those experiences. From being bold enough to wear your natural hair to speaking up when someone mispronounces your name, know that our melanin is greater than being deemed a minority in any forum. Always remember to play the game, and document statements of discrimination, acts of injustice, and exclusion. When looking for employment, place your mental health before your desire for money as a toxic work environment will cause you to be dissatisfied no matter the paycheck. Our **Melanin** is greater than the workplace!

Takeaway with you these Melanin How To's to use whenever you are looking for a new job, starting a business, or want to implement your melanin into your current position.

1. Familiarize yourself with your company's policies to prevent discrmination tactics used through policy.
2. Respond to unnecessary criticism with your WHY at the forefront of your mind. Ex. Why am I here?
3. Document all interactions that you feel to be inappropriate with the date, time, and incident. Keep this log so that you have records of proof.

4. Keep in mind your goals and control your emotions to prevent disqualifying yourself from opportunities.
5. Code-switching can be beneficial but also exhausting, it requires a balance.
6. Remember that passion is often viewed as argumentative or intimidation to white people.
7. Never assume anything of someone just because their melanin matches yours.
8. Always give a hand up to a fellow person of color!
9. Your ethnicity can benefit you, always negotiate your pay to include the service of translation if you want to use it!
10. Cultural competency and inclusiveness is mandatory of an employer.
11. Our Melanin cannot dictate the choices we make, only we as individuals can do that!

12. Mental health is important, they don't get to add to our insecurities.
13. Networking is a person of color's best way to build capital as an entrepreneur.

Works Cited

Bilall Fallah, Michael Bay, Adil El Arbi, Columbia Pictures, *Bad Boys, 1995[Film]*

Bloomberg city lab.2018. *Why Entrepreneurs of Color are Struggling.* https://www.bloomberg.com/news/articles/2018-04-23/4-ways-to-help-close-the-racial-startup-gap

CNN. "Teen who wore Mexican flag at graduation gets the diploma he was denied at the ceremony."*CNN © 2022 Cable News Network. A Warner Media Company. All Rights Reserved. CNN Sans ™ & © 2016 Cable News Network.* https://www.cnn.com/2021/06/08/us/mexican-student-denied-diploma-flag-trnd/index.html.

Google.Definition of Professionalism
https://www.google.com/search?q=definition+of+professionalism&rlz=1C1CHBF_enUS940US941&sxsrf=AOaemvI5kscd-eQ-EemPC6YvJcaeIO4tRg%3A1642431801310&ei=OYXlY

Definition of Code-switching

https://www.jopwell.com/thewell/posts/how-code-switching-in-the-workplace-has-been-normalized-for-pocs

https://www.pdfprof.com/PDF_Image.php?idt=71675&t=28

Indeed. 2021.
https://www.indeed.com/career/translator/salaries

NPR.What it means to be called a sell out.2008.
https://www.npr.org/sections/talk/2008/02/what_it_means_to_be_called_a_s.html

Popsugar interview, 2018, Women in the world interview (Viola Davis)
https://www.popsugar.com/celebrity/viola-davis-v

iral-women-in-the-world-interview-video-475884 35

M.Rotenberg & I. Rae.2016-2021.Insecure. Season 1, Episode 3

The Network Journal, July 9,2021
https://tnj.com/why-do-black-owned-businesses-fail/

About the Author

Janae Grimball grew up an Army brat. She currently lives in Atlanta, GA with her husband and their three sons. Sharmel enjoys watching movies, meditating, traveling, and spending time with her family and friends. She has a Master's degree in Child Development and a Bachelor's degree in Crisis Counseling from Liberty University. Sharmel is a first-time author who was inspired by her experiences in the workplace to write this book. As a Black businesswoman, she encountered frequent discrimination and disadvantages to being a person of color in the workplace. Despite her challenges, she overcame them and knew that she had to pass on the information that helped her be successful to other people of color.

Subscribe For Updates and Other Exclusive Content At:

www.authorofuncomfortabletruths.com

Janae is available for workshops, conferences and diversity consultations which can also be booked on her website.

Follow Our Social Media Pages for live discussions and more Uncomfortable Truths with the author at:

IG:@author.of.uncomfortable.truths
FB:@authorofuncomfortabletruths

The Next Uncomfortable Truth Coming Soon:
The Selfish Mommy

I remember the day I chose to be selfish, the day I chose myself over my children and husband. It was Veterans Day and my job was officially closed for the day. I was so excited to have a day to myself that I booked the day full of spa and self care activities.

I started my morning with a cup of hot lemon ginger tea, prayed, meditated and made my way to my 11 o'clock appointment for a hot stone massage. I was even looking forward to my first Brazilian wax that I scheduled for myself after much hesitation.

The day is mine, I told myself, as soon as I entered the parking lot, my phone began to ring. I looked at the number and knew right away it was one of my kids' schools. I briefly contemplated not answering but thought what the hell maybe it's nothing.

"Hello," I said with hesitation.

"Hi Mrs. Grimball, this is the nurse at Bear Creek Middle, I believe we spoke yesterday," she said in a condescending tone. "I'm here with your son and he is complaining of a sore throat and a headache. Can you please come pick him up?"

I sank into my car's leather seat with a major attitude, "um, does he have a fever?

"No, his temperature was normal 98.6."

"Okay, when did his throat start hurting? I spoke to him this morning and he was fine. Can I speak to him please?"

I tried to calm myself before going off.

Why didn't you tell me you didn't feel well when you woke up this morning? You did this yesterday and you were fine. Why should I miss out on my self care to run back to the other side of town to pick him up when he's probably fine?

All these thoughts were racing through my head until I heard my son's voice snap me out of it.

"Mommy?"

"Isaiah, what's bothering you?"

"My throat and head hurts."

"Since when Isaiah? You usually tell me you aren't feeling well before you leave the house in the morning. Why didn't you ?"

"I don't know why I didn't."

"Okay sweetie. Put the nurse back on the phone. Ma'am," I said aggravated, "can you please give him a cough drop?"

"No, we are not allowed to give anything to the children. You can bring him some to the school."

"Okay, I have appointments that I have to attend today so I can't drop everything and come right now. Let me see if I can call his grandma or my husband to pick him up."

Before I knew it I had hung up the phone and pressed my head onto my steering wheel holding back tears.

I'm not canceling this appointment! They would charge me for canceling this late anyway. I told myself. I immediately called my husband's work phone.

"Hello?"

"Babe, I'm trying not to get frustrated."

"What's wrong ?"

"The school just called, Isaiah is complaining of a sore throat and a headache. The school wants me to pick him up and I'm not doing it! I finally have a day for me and I'm not missing this appointment. Can you leave work and get him? If not, I can get him after my massage."

I felt bad asking my husband to leave work, lose money for our household just so I could get a massage. But I quickly told myself, "No! My body needs this and there has to be another way for it to get resolved other than me having to sacrifice something." I was in such a deep conversation with myself I barely noticed my husband responding.

"Yea, babe I can leave work, drop him off at home and come back. Go enjoy your massage."

"Are you sure?" I said, full of guilt, "will your boss be fine with it?"

"Yea, I'm fine baby I'm leaving now."

I sighed a huge sigh of relief! Thank God I'm no longer a single mother, and thank God my husband has my back!

I rushed into my appointment, tried to clear my mind and relax but I couldn't. My mind was racing, why did Isaiah have to pull this stunt today, of all days! My one day for me ? The nurse probably thinks I'm a shitty mother for not running over to the school without hesitation. If only she knew how much I always give up she wouldn't think that.I caught myself and realized that I wasn't enjoying the massage at all because I was dealing with that damn mommy guilt!

I quickly took a deep breath and told myself, "relax, it has been handled. Your husband is taking care of it. You don't have to be involved in everything. Right?"

Why does choosing myself over my child feel so damn horrible even when he is taken care of by his other parent? Why did I feel like it should have been me?

www.ingramcontent.com/pod-product-compliance
Lightning Source LLC
Chambersburg PA
CBHW022115090426
42743CB00008B/863